Dorothy Porter has established an international reputation as one of Australia's most exciting and innovative writers. Born in Sydney in 1954, she graduated from Sydney University in 1975, the same year as her first collection of poetry, *Little Hoodlum*, was published. Attaining a Diploma of Education, she supported her writing by part-time teaching for a number of years, before becoming a lecturer in Poetry and Writing at the University of Technology, Sydney. Her verse crime thriller, *The Monkey's Mask*, has become an international bestseller.

Dorothy Porter currently lives in Melbourne, where she is working on a new verse novel.

**Also by Dorothy Porter and published
by Serpent's Tail**

The Monkey's Mask

'To be relished as Byron was devoured by contemporary
fans, canto by furious canto.' *Literary Review*

'The most remarkable first novel I have read this year.'
Val McDermid, *Manchester Evening News*

'A beautiful, slippery, wholly felt epic of love, betrayal
and murder that you have to restrain yourself from
reading at a sitting.' *Independent*

'Sensational… A book to rave about, to gasp at the
daring, the beauty – and the wit.' *Australian Bookseller
& Publisher*

'You don't read this, you experience it. It does things
to you.' *Sydney Morning Herald*

Akhenaten

DOROTHY PORTER

Library of Congress Catalog Card Number: 98-88359

A catalogue record for this book is available from the
British Library on request

The right of Dorothy Porter to be identified as the author
of this work has been asserted by her in accordance with
the Copyright, Designs and Patents Act 1988

First published in 1992 by University of Queensland Press
Second edition published in 1998 by
Hyland House Publishing Pty Limited, Australia

First published in 1999 by
Serpent's Tail, 4 Blackstock Mews, London N4
Website: www.serpentstail.com

Printed in Great Britain by Mackays of Chatham, plc

10 9 8 7 6 5 4 3 2 1

For my mother, Jean,
and also my grandmother,
Mary Fabian Featherstone.

"To speak the name of the dead
is to make them live again."

(Egyptian Funerary Inscription)

CONTENTS

Akhet-Aten
Regnal Years 6-12

Notes

ACKNOWLEDGMENTS

Some of these poems have appeared in *Meanjin* (Writers in the Park issue), *Pictures from an Exhibition* (Mattara Poetry Prize Anthology 1989), *Editions*, and *Salt*.

My primary source has been the work of the notable Egyptologist, Cyril Aldred, in particular his *Akhenaten* (Abacus 1972) and *Akhenaten* (Thames and Hudson 1988). In some instances I have drawn my own conclusions from his invaluable research.

I would also like to thank Lyn Hughes for her generous editorial contributions.

This work was assisted by a writer's grant from the Australia Council, the Federal Government's arts funding and advisory body.

INTRODUCTION
TO THE FIRST EDITION

Akhenaten was king of Egypt from 1378 B.C. to 1362 B.C. I first saw him in a museum in West Berlin in 1976. I had come to see the famous bust of his wife, Nefertiti, but it was the smirking, distorted, oddly beautiful face of Akhenaten that put out tentacles to my imagination. A strange confession from a feminist poet.

Akhenaten would have been an anomaly in the history of any country. He is credited with establishing the world's first monotheistic religion—the worship of Aten represented by the Sun Disk. He was a visionary and poet. To celebrate his religious revolution he initiated and encouraged an equally bold adventure in the arts. He was fascinated with himself, ecstatically aware of his own uniqueness. His family life, including his love for wife Nefertiti, his six daughters and his younger brother, Smenkhkare, was illustrated in painting, inscription and sculpture all over Egypt. For a profoundly conservative people like the ancient Egyptians, comfortable with a relatively static culture thousands of years old, it was all too much.

Akhenaten only ruled for seventeen years. In that time he smashed the tolerant and flexible pantheon of gods and goddesses, insisting in his last years, with all the fanaticism of an iconoclast, that only Aten could be worshipped. He removed the seat of government from Thebes to his new city, Akhet-Aten, where he isolated himself and his court and let the running of the kingdom slide into military neglect and economic ruin. On his death he was execrated as a heretic, his name removed from monuments, his city abandoned and used as a quarry. The old gods, notably, Amun, the powerful god of Thebes, were restored to their past wealth and glory. The Egyptians wanted to forget the heady Akhenaten years as quickly as possible.

In 1987 I began writing this book. In 1989 I went to Egypt and stood before his colossal hermaphroditic statue in the Cairo Museum. A week later I stood on the emphatically laid out foundations of his city, now known as Tell el Amarna. Nearby a mourning wheatear, flickered its black and white tail on the stone stump of a temple column. Akhenaten always said the souls of the dead came back as birds.

Dorothy Porter
3rd April 1991
Mount Victoria

INTRODUCTION
TO THIS EDITION

Outside it's not Egypt. I'm looking at a playing field coated with frost. In the distance there are the magnificent stone spires of Cambridge. It's a ripe English autumn and the trees are moulting showers of golden and red leaves. The light is a faintly pearly blue, very gentle on the eyes. It's not Egypt.

But it's here, yesterday, at the Fitzwilliam Museum, that I stared again into Pharaoh Akhenaten's hypnotic stone face. It had been mutilated. It was a tantalising fragment, just a hint of his old head. His enemies had smashed away his swollen forehead, his narrow eyes, his fine aristocratic nose. The marks of their determination to totally obliterate this heretic king, this detested iconoclast, are still plain. It reminded me how much this man had been hated. His freakish, explosively creative, regime lasted a mere seventeen years—a speck on the rolling millenia of Egyptian dynastic history.

There's something almost viral about Akhenaten's face. You only need to be exposed to it briefly and it will replicate itself potently in your mind. His face, safely in the museum cabinet, with only lips and chin intact, was infecting me again. It's his smirking mouth, lush with arrogance. For seventeen years he had and did it all.

I finished writing this book seven years ago and I thought I'd finished with Akhenaten, Pharaoh, beloved of the Sun God Aten, visionary poet, ardent husband of Nefertiti, designer and builder of a jerry-built dream city, enemy of the Gods, pervert and megalomaniac. Like his enemies, I underestimated his lingering, obstinate charm. He's back.

Dorothy Porter
30th October 1997
Cambridge

MALKATA

I Survived

I've always known
my enemies.

When I was a child
Amun had the better of me.

I was little Horseface
with the wheezing lungs
and the wet bed.

Amun threw me down
in drooling, pissing fits.

I was only a second son
they all thought I'd die

Amun would climb
on my face
and spread his black bum
over my eyes and mouth

I thought he'd choke me

while my older brother
Tutmose
swanned around Karnak
in white linen

Amun loved him.

But one day
my parents gave me
Aten
like you'd throw a child
drinking from a street sewer
a slice of honey bread

I gorged on my God
I swelled up huge

that year
Tutmose shrivelled up
and died

I survived.

4

Malkata

Incense and myrrh!

my nose
takes me back

Incense and myrrh!

Mother walks towards me
through the painted water
of Malkata

and for her
those blue tiles
roll back

Incense and myrrh!

purr around us
like throngs of invisible
scented cats

Mother rattling
with huge jewellery

her necklace
catches me on the nose

Ouch!

We laugh
Mother and I
my voice
squeaks high and excited
like a jack donkey
downwind of a jenny

but she keeps laughing
with me
even when her slaves stare

incense and myrrh!

I'll never clear
Malkata or Mother
from my nose.

Cat-Nap

In my father's harem
I lie on the mosaic fish floor
his filmy women
   float around me.

Nofret, my fat old queen,
snoring
   like a humming toy
   her paw
     curled
       on my throat.

We sleep together
   through the prattle
   through the sticky afternoon.

My father's stupid.

I will collect cats
   not princesses.

Nofret

I wouldn't let Nofret
go fowling
with Ay and his friends
in the marshes
near Malkata

she was my own
tubby speckled cat
who moaned in her fat sleep
at the end of my bed
her soft twitching weight
sometimes on my bare feet

she liked food and sleep
if she were a goddess
she was an easy one
though greedy one
to please

but a bull hippo
would have moved
more delicately
over the lily pads
to retrieve ducks
for the hunters
than my Nofret.

My Best Friend

It was Nefertiti
who stayed with me
the hot night
    they found Nofret

down in the reeds
her eyes full of ants
her stink
    made my mother turn her head

it was Nefertiti
who let me talk
myself out
and held me
while I bawled
    stinging snotty tears

my tiny cousin
whose brains and beauty
cut everyone down to size
cleaned me up
    and became my best friend.

My Mother

My mother is a politician

and a good one

she loves power
she loves paper-work

that edge
that knot in her lip
    can send a scribe
        or general
            to the pot
                with a griping gut!

my father plays
    in his inoffensive way
with his health
    or his harem

Mummy plays
    with gods
Mummy frightens
    iron.

Mother's
New God

You don't cross Mother.

When Leopard Spots
didn't ask her
to play Mut
on the Sacred Lake
in some bit of priests' theatre

she never forgot.

The special lake
my father dug out
just for her
all the fuss
even a ceremonial scarab

none of it was enough

Mother always knew
a sop
especially if it came
with fanfare
from my father
who could order her
a lake
but couldn't order
Amun
to let her play Mut.

Years later
Mother told me
she wanted a god
on side

this was always
her idea of worship

but, still,
she let Aten
loose
in my baby head.

11

His Favourite Food

I can't move.

I've sent Ipy
and my other slaves
    away.

I don't have marsh fever
don't get Mother.

This morning
my bones could snap
    like charred sticks
I can smell Aten
    on my breath

He's cooking me
    alive!

Am I His sacrificial ox
    barbecuing slowly
for the relish
    of His famished nose?

I will make a frazzled king.

Priests And Cobras

Even as kids
we knew.

Nefertiti,
her eyes like hawks,
once dug me in the ribs,

'That priest of Amun
    just farted
in the presence of your Dad
look at him cackling
he did it on purpose
he's lucky your Mum's
    not around!'

As usual
my father was vaguely smiling
    and handing out gold necklaces.

That royal cobra
    lifeless on his plump head
I'd teach it to spit.

Heliopolis

The first time I saw
Nefer-re
he was standing before
the alabaster table of Herakhte
in his panther skin
placing lotus flowers
over the wine jugs

his hands
slow as a scribe's

he never rushed anything

he told me
that to the penetrating mind
there was only one God
but Herakhte welcomed strangers
no matter what gods
they served
no matter what names
they called them

we all glitter
under the disk of the Sun
he said

but for those three months
no one glittered
like Nefer-re

I kept him from his duties

he drew me triangles
that pricked
with their empty
mysterious tips

I imagined myself
dead in one
and Nefer-re's clever face
unravelling over me
in grief

before I went home
I gave him a triangle
of solid gold

but he remained
    unpenetrated.

The Lion

Somewhere in the desert
there is a lion

its spine crushed
under chariot wheels
arrows
    in its bleeding eyes!

it's yowling
    in my skull

the lion
    kicks and jerks in the sand
    it won't die

Aten,
    don't You care
    who dies slowly?

am I brave enough
to let You
mince me under Your wheels?

Amun's Sanctuary

In the only bit of light
in this dark old room
the High Priest changes
Amun's dirty nappy
and tries to force
fine bites of meat, duck
and honey
down the god's metal throat

my father's eyes are streaming
in the smoke of incense
and burning blood

'Stop smirking'
he whispers solemnly
so the priests will think
he's sharing a prayer
with his young son
the Horus-in-Waiting

they bow their oiled scalps
to our intimate piety

look, Dad,
I'm not sneering at your gods
I feel sick
can't we leave
this idol's hole
just for a minute
    and stand in the Sun?

My Fifteenth Birthday

My parents gave me
 a senet set.

It's played
 on an ebony stand
 that looks like a black cat
 with neat gold paws

she's so nice to touch

before I go to sleep
I lean out
 find her in the dark
and stroke
 her smooth legs

I can hear
 her black purr

I've called her
 Mutje

who cares
if no woman
 ever wants to stroke me.

Our First Time

I can't stop shaking
    or laughing

she's as silly as me

and her lips
are swollen and wet

I can't stop kissing her

when her tongue filled
    my mouth
for the first time
my cock went berserk
it wouldn't listen

now it flops sticky
and happy
    in her hand

and I'm not embarrassed!

she's still
    my best friend.

My First Cup Of Wine

Ay gave me my first cup of wine
   not my father
it was chilled
spices swam in it
   like hot little fish.

He watched me
   with my mother's eyes
but didn't speak
I asked for more
he poured it
as if I were my father.

We were sitting by my mother's lake
Aten was banging the water
   making it spark
the wine sang in my gut
I told Ay everything

he bowed his head
yes, Ay did,
his hard chin touched his chest
he told me
I would teach him
he would serve me

   I would be his God.

THEBES

Regnal Years 1–6

My
Co-Regency
Coronation

My father's breath stinks
under the Double Crown

his old face creased with toothache
under the bobbing cobra

while the droning flies of Memphis
crown me
I watch his pudgy hands tremble
for poppy juice, a dark room
and my mother's cool sense

afterwards
with love
I tell him
to leave this bad air
and lay his head
    in the lap of Aten.

That's Him

Ay,
write this down.

On the new temple walls
Aten will have a new cartouche.

Ready?

'Re-Herakhte,
rejoicing on the Horizon
in His manifestation
of the Light
that is in the Sun Disk
Aten
the Living
the Great
Who is in Jubilee
Lord of Heaven and Earth.'

Yes, in Jubilee!
Aten has honours and feasts
to catch up
He shall have them all
immediately.
Amun struts around
with all his baubles
like a Syrian's kept boy!

Aten will have a new sign

He is not a falcon
He makes falcons
He will be drawn
as the Sun Disk
encircled by a uraeus

befitting the Father of the King
then an ankh
from which will descend
at least a dozen rays
ending in hands
giving his breath
first to me
then my queen
then our daughter

explain—no—
show
Bek and the others
what I want

There, Ay,
that's Him
that's Aten
simple, perfect

the one true God.

Like No One Else

You don't look awful

Nefertiti says

you don't look like anyone else
in the world

only a god could have
your face

that's why people stare

do you want to be ordinary?

only Aten could have made you

you don't look like
your parents

take your hands away
show the Two Lands

what a wonder you are.

By Royal Decree

I am a dance
you will learn

I am the cliff
you will leap

I am lover's breath

you will break off
in my sweet hand

you will come together
on my hot breast

you will know me
you will know God.

Fits

Suddenly

your ka is snatched

and when it wanders
    back to you
mute and white-eyed

it can't tell you
    what happened.

Aten,
    teach me
    how to live with them.

My Statues

Bek's my pet sculptor.
He does what he's told
like any inspired artist.

I wanted my statues
for the temple at Karnak
to be the mirrors
of my terrible ka.

Let my kingdom
stand in their shadows
and see the God I mate.

Bek watched me draw for him
my ka's belly and groin
in the sand,
my stick trembling.

Is that you, Pharaoh?
He said and his voice
shivered.

My headache under
the black sun started
and I held my hot hands
to my eyes
and I said

give me a beautiful mouth
for Nefertiti
but the rest—

and I finished the ka's gross
breasts and swollen thighs
in the nauseating sand—
is as I'm showing you

this is who I am.

My White Queen

My wife wears a fighter's crown
as she sings beside me
in the temple
growling the words
in her lion's contralto

her cheek at my shoulder
but her teeth in my heart
her hand taps my leg
in time with the sistrum
like the tip of a restless spear

Aten has fired my queen
in His whitest ray.

My Temple

In my temple
there are no roofs
Aten lifts me by the nose
with His fresh air
with His shining hand.

Behind me
Nefertiti sniffs Aten's Hands
and sways with Their mead scent.

Behind her
our precious daughter, Merytaten,
shakes the sistrum
and grows ripe.

Nefertiti
Rides Me

Nefertiti rides me.

Her cunt
   slippery on
      the hot skin
         of my belly.

She's sticky
   with my glue—
      that high stink
       of seed!

My tongue
   tastes her sap
     a sweat-honey
       shot with salt
still wild
   in the corners of my
      mouth.

I want to hold her
I want to lie still
but she's not finished
   her eyes are shut
   her breath
     a stammering breeze
now, now
   oh, yes

she growls like the desert
   melts like sleep
     and anoints me
       exquisitely.

I'm her war horse
she looks down
   from hooded eyes
and laughs, laughs.

I love her more than Aten.

God-Watching

I watch the morning ritual
of Thoth, the sacred ibis.

He grooms his feathers
with his fussing hook beak
then shits
with a quick squirt
on a library of papyrus.

Strange behaviour
for the god of scribes!

My Ka

My ka has big breasts
that can squirt milk as far
as Kush.

My ka has fat thighs
as heavy as gold.

She hides her cock
but can flash for
ceremonial occasions.

My ka built statues of herself
for the temple at Karnak
and the priests wondered how
I fathered my children.

My ka gives me sunstroke.
She stakes me out
in a noon fire.

I don't fight her.

Family Life And Furnaces

While walking
  by the lake
that my father made for my mother
    Meri wants me to catch
      a green-gold frog
      basking on a lily-pad.
For her it's a pet scarab.
I slowly
  reach out my hand
    (my hand! so fine.
  The only part of me
    not ugly.
  My Nefertiti loves my hands
  arches like a tight bow
  when I stroke her breasts.)
but the frog
  scares
leaping
  without even rippling the water
from pad to pad
  with an easy, graceful magic.

Like my times with Aten
when I walk unharmed
  in His furnace
and even my shadow
is comfortable
  and cool.
I walk on fire
  without making a ripple.

No-one knows how I do it.

AKHET-ATEN

Regnal Years 6–12

The 13th Day
Of The
8th Month
Of The 6th Year

I watch
Aten being born
in the spreading blood
of the horizon

a shining child
He'll come to my scented tent
call me to my gold chariot
and ride behind me
hugging my waist
while We name the boundaries
of His City.

Aten,
this day is too hot
to touch

the cliffs are bowing to us
the desert has laid out
a carpet embossed
with burning stones

I can't look at it

instead, my God,
I'll drive blind
my horses, Your horses
Your Light, my light.

In My Ka's Eye

Tired
I stare at the sand
between my new boundary stones.

I could be Hatshepsut
gawking at the fat royal family
of Punt
I could be a peasant
spying a pissed priest of Amun
piddling behind the god's veils
at the Inundation Festival
I could be my eldest daughter
watching me hesitate to club
a duck in the reeds
I could be myself at any time
seeing Nefertiti's succulent mouth.

I stare now at nothing
I stare at featureless sand

but my mouth waters
at the delectable city
in my ka's eye.

Inundation

Aten has sung to the Nile
  early this year

the Black Land is under water
and the peasants
are hammering my new city
stealing piece by piece
from the infatuated Red Land

both the Black
and the Red Lands
of my kingdom
tremble for Aten
do His bidding
like a twelve-year-old bride
in His harem rooms

but then
Aten trembles for me
or do I tremble for Him?

Sometimes He is imperious,
shoves me away
and I lie prostrate
among the cool mosaic water lilies
hysterically immobile
as any woman
blubbering ignored
on the harem floor.

But other times
He calls for me
silly with desire
whimpering
the Black and Red Lands
adore Me
why don't you?

And then
I switch my lion's tail
in His face
and have His dawn for dinner.

Flash Flood

In Akhet-Aten
we'll paint water
on everything

the palace floor
the temple walls
everything
from the peasant's pitcher
to the crown
on my queen's head
I want everything
splashed blue

this will be
my flash flood

in its wake
my city will shimmer
along the river
like wet silk.

Wrapped in it
I will entertain my God.

Luminous

My mouth
  spiced with sunlight

luminous

what a tasty word!

the juice
  of a fresh melon

the spiked drink
  of an erect nipple

luminous

my mouth sends Aten
  incense.

I Lay Out My Pens

I've had a lovely morning
wasting time

I walked down to the river
with Meri
who painted me
a blue duck

I lingered over
breakfast with my wife
who looks gorgeous
smeared with melon juice

then Parenefer poured me
a jar of beer
that got bottomless
during his fart concert
oh, I pissed myself
laughing
at his anal rendition
of Amun's Sed Hymn

even Ay cracked
a smile
saying that Old Pa
was a silly old fart himself
but certainly very musical!

But Pa's Hymn
reminded me
I had work to do
my own Hymn to write

so here I am

my gut full of beer
my eyes wet from laughing
trying to compose myself
into composing
a Hymn for the temple
a Hymn for the city
a Hymn for my people
a Hymn for my wonderful God

I lay out my pens
and pick my ear
there's something out the window
a donkey
his black penis extended
a happy erection in the sun

I watch him for luck
and let my Hymn come.

Hymn To
The Sun

You who are born
beautiful
on the horizon of the world
You who are first born
rising in the East
You feed every land
Your beauty
You dazzle us
You who shine high above us
with Your rays
that flood the land
to the very end of all
You have made

All the animals delight
in their fields
You make the trees and the gardens
lush and green
birds leap and fly from their nests
the cattle skip on their hooves
everything that flies comes to life
when You wake up

How myriad is the world
You have made

You are the sole God
There is no other like You
You made the world
as You pleased
All alone You made everything
on earth that walks and flies

When You rise
Your rays pour into the fields
that live and grow for You
You made the seasons succour
the whole of Your creation
Your cool hand in winter
Your taste in summer

No-one knows You
save Your son, Akhenaten
who is Your Beloved.

Smenkhkare Is Fourteen

Smenkhkare is fourteen.

He eats with his mouth open
puts his growing feet
    all over the furniture
and badgers me
    with his stupid questions.

Mother is too busy
too impatient
she lets him
drive me mad
    his big singing voice
        cracking
    all over the palace.

His nose
    in my things
or sniffing in my ear
while I'm composing poems
    for the glory of Aten.

So cheeky
when I shout at him
he wipes his nose with his hand
then connives for my pardon
    and a slobbering hug.

Mother,
    he's your problem.
Take him to Malkata!

The True World

Aten is not a mirror

He bastes my eyes
with the true world
not reflection, not shadow

the fish, the chick, the grit of sand
all swim together
and sparkle with equal light
as motes
in Aten's rushing seed.

Geese In
A Harp

Roast geese
   can fly too
I watch their aroma
   flap
      to the blue ceiling

I ground one
   with a deep bite
   on its golden drumstick

while the rest
   in a formation of herbs
   flock in the sky notes
      of a plucked harp.

I pick my teeth
to the loveliest music.

Full Moon

Why do you love the moon so much,
  my beautiful queen?

For me
  your eyes, your mouth,
  give off far more light.

There's no heat
  in the moon,
it's no god
it's just the black sky
playing with Aten's little mirror
while He's asleep.

But, yes, I'm enjoying this cool toy
  tonight
as it flickers blue and silver
over your breasts

just as
your hard nipple
  blisters my tongue.

My Way

Is to ride
like a holy hoon
through my own city
planned, built and blessed
by me

bare skin, ribbons flying
cuddling my wife.

Is to throw down
golden goodies
necklaces or scraps of roast duck
to friend and crawler alike
from the Window of Appearances
with a giggle and a wave
and an improvised poem.

No, I'm not a sandstone mummy
carved with moronic serenity
on a temple wall.

Look at me
I'm a marvel
and so embarrassing!

The Hot Ant

Aten is creeping
across my writing hand

like a hot ant

He tickles me

into the hottest man
who has ever written.

My Daughter's Skull

My right hand
  cups the skull
of my three-week-old daughter
  Ankhesenpaaten
her veins flutter
  beneath the silky fuzz.

My fingers measure
  another long skull
    in the family,
all my girls
  have Aten's eggs for heads,
their mother and I
  just brood hens
  protecting them
  while they hatch.

This is Ankhesenpaaten's egg skull
  poised between my hand
    and the ankh
      in Aten's hand
that will crack it open.

Hoopoe

Meri wants one for a pet

to wobble behind her on a string
bright orange, bright black
its comb pulled up and down

for once
I've said No

I like them in my garden

I stop when I see one

its silly head
fills mine

hoopoe
is all I can say

Roses

A dark rose
   floats
in a bowl
   of light water

its scent creeps
   like a slow spider
   up my face

and it stings
   in the eyes

so I cry
   for pleasure
   for no reason
       in Nefertiti's rose room.

Sauce

My love said to me
'Now I know what
a woman tastes like'

she prowled over
to me like a queen
temple cat

'the sea'

I ran my knuckles
slowly down her face
my naughty
my sauce-for-the-goose
Nefertiti

I asked her what they'd
talked about

'Our children!'

Did she recognise you?

'No. And she faked
an orgasm for me.
Very touching
she made so much noise!'

Did you come?

'Oh, she would have
made Osiris come.'

What did she do to you?

'She stroked me with ebony
she sucked me like an oyster
so professional.'

Then my wife
with her white hands
drew for me
in the air
the room
and the whore's ornaments.

Did she get many women clients?

Nefertiti laughed.

'I was her first.'

Married Gods

I walk behind
my glowing belly

and the sea parts
for my huge child

I am a swollen Sun
waddling across the sky

my child swims in me
kicking at my bladder

heads turn, old prayers wither
in the heat of this pregnant man

slim Nefertiti glides
through the city laughing

my queen and I
can do anything.

Those Sandals

I told Nefertiti not
to wear those sandals

she loves them
she won't listen to me

they flick silver about
as she walks

but she slips on them
every few steps

my darling's pregnant again
she won't listen to me

this afternoon
she was walking behind me
down the path
to a pleasure kiosk by the river

I had my hands full
six-month-old Ankhie
wriggling in my arms
twisting her head
to hoot in my neck

my wife
carrying Meketaten
who should have been walking

I told her she'd slip

a slave had to lift my wife
to her feet

I have two hands
not Aten's hundreds

she won't listen to me

tonight
she limps
beside me to dinner
in those sandals.

Aten's Scent

Aten can't die

He will not grow black
in the fug of a tomb tunnel

every morning
He kicks away
my kohl, my wigs
and my burnt down
wax cones

He splashes cold light
in my face
and I take His scent
deep in my lungs
the aroma of grass
under the dawn moon

62

Dancing On Light

Light.

It's just after sunrise.

And I dance on light
    I dance on a sword
    that breaks

everywhere.

Dawn over Akhet-Aten.

Peace.
    I give peace
    to my city

dancing on light

    on sunlight.

Live Art

Why does the musician
play with closed eyes?

What can he see
inside his sightless music
that he can't show me?
I watch the red and green fish
swim in a wall frieze,
but they are glittering dry
     not live wet.

I am a creative God;
so I fashion a quick fish
out of bread and bits of chicken
then free it
in a lake of wine
to catch soaking wet
with my jaws crocodile-wide.

My daughters laugh
and choke on their food.

The musician stops playing
his ears turning like annoyed eyes
looking for the disruption.

At The High Altar

Not now.
Not this minute.
Not before the high altar.

My bladder
swelling
about to bust a canal

oh, to be a dirty peasant
pissing at the mud!

and Meryre fingering
his gold collars
(the ones I threw him)
watching me
as he drones my Hymn

the words go on forever
did I write it?

distract myself
yes, the daytime full moon
amazing like a fat pearl
over the purple cliffs

steam
from the calf's cut throat
flowers, flowers

fresh and wet
Aten's finickity Hands
picking through them

Meryre has never sung
this badly, this slowly,
the bastard!
my bladder prods me
to sing faster.

The New Temple

'Are you counting my ribs?'

My brother looks over
his bare shoulder

Only sixteen.

I was watching
the new hard curve
of his bent back
as he planes the wood
for a pleasure boat

he's so good with his hands

my old hands
    dangle
like trawled octopus
good for nothing
but sex, prayers
    and scribbling

it's his back
that makes me stare
like a wall-eyed priest
at the glinting stone
    of a new temple.

Watching Hippos

I like the rhythm
of hippos

the wide ripples
they make in the water
that spread
like a run of smooth honey
right into the reeds

they know
I won't hunt them

they blow near my boat
their snorting nose spray
then roll silently
in the water
disappearing

till a lump with bulging eyes
tells me they're back

I watch them all afternoon
rocking on their swell

their huge undulating presence
refreshes me better
than sleep.

Penehse's Tomb

This is taking forever

Penehse's prattle
his winy breath
tickling my ear

the horse is drunk too
stumbling on every second stone

the cliffs glow blueish
but don't get any closer
as we trip, lurch
and talk, talk
across this flat of desert

to see his tomb
to bless its progress

'Son of Aten'
he says for the 93rd time

'I am so honoured
I can barely speak!'

for your sake, Penehse,
I wish that were true

your yapping is chipping out
in my inner ear
another deeper tomb for you!

Death And A Randy Vulture

It's all rubbish

but I still enjoy
the dirty joke
in the Osiris story

there he lies
mangled
stinking with death
swaddled in bandages

then in comes
Eset the Vulture
licking her chops
at this delectable stiff

and something rises at her
that's hornier
than the smell
of old blood and nitron

the biggest prick
she's ever seen
tearing through the mummy cloths
like a red hungry beak

its eye stares at her
as lidless as a cobra's
but Osiris is dead
no breath lifts his bandages
his chest is still
but his prick is swaying
like a charmed snake!

What is a poor vulture to do
eat it or fuck it?

Stomach and cunt
have a civil discussion.

The prick is such a lovely purple
the colour of ripe carrion
cunt wins

and Horus
is conceived.

I'll Enjoy
Shrivelling Up

Aten can't help himself—

he gnaws everything
    in the end
yellow
    down to roots
    down to sand

and not even slaps
    of Nile mud
can save you.

But I'll enjoy
    shrivelling up

in the end
I'll run finer
    than powdered sand
and fly everywhere.

Silver
Jewellery

Aten smelts the Nile
to silver

drifting downstream
I make jewellery
effortlessly
with my trailing hand

jewellery
like no animal seen
like no god imagined

my underwater fingers
are craftsmen
are priests!

until Any pesters me
with paperwork

I'll wipe my dripping hands
on his new wig.

Drunk

We don't count each other's drinks
my wife and I

wine travels
so I'm singing
about a journey
in a gold barque
to the Sun
where I melt

melting legs
I sit down
shut up
and squint at the food

a melting fish
looks at me
with my mother's fixed eye
I blind it
with a date
wipe my fingers
on Nefertiti's banqueting breasts

under the Sun
I melt
when I go places.

Ankhie's Lion

Ankhie,
  I did look properly.

I swear by my dusty nose
there's no lion under your bed.

Sekhmet hasn't made you sick
she's just a stone

you could smash
her lion head
right off her shoulders
if you tried

don't let stone roar at you
my big, strong girl

roar back.

Afternoon In
The Oasis

At the edge
of the green canal
an egret steps
through its own reflection

a donkey brays
like a yawn
under a palm

Nefertiti stops our driver
and we walk
through our shadows
under the frish
of fans.

Painted Ponds

This morning
I fell onto the painted pond
of my palace floor

my head cracked
splashing the lotuses

that splashed me back
with a drenching of scent

Nefertiti called the servants
who put me to bed
muttering charms

instead they should
have picked the duck-down
from my fallen wig.

My Girls As Wall Painting

They skitter together
on the wall
   like sibling kittens

my little girls
   Neferneferuaten and Neferneferure
what a mouthful
   naming them after their mother!

they play in their lovely skins
   beads and bangles
the sting of their glossy eyes!

on my bedroom wall
   my tiny idols live forever.

Kiya

When Nefertiti
   is sick of me

I spend the night
   with Kiya

she sets out my food
   and warms my cup
   in her plump small hands

I sprawl
   over the table
talk
   with my mouth full
and don't pretend
   an interest
   in her concerns

so restful
to be the beloved
of a secondary wife.

Kingfishers

You want a war, Horemheb?
Well, let's test your manhood
in the marshes.

Take cover!
those blue arrows
really fly
and can slice your cheek
or stab your eyeball.

Fearless arrows
not made of copper
watch the Sun
pick out the flash
of a mysterious blue metal
(even the Hittites can't make it)
as they swoop and dive.

Those arrows are birds, General,
they won't snap in two
nor can you chop off
their archer's hands.

So taunt them with a fish
they'll give you a good fight
just leave me in peace.

My Father's Black Hands

When the embalmers
   have finished with him
under the bandages
   my father's hands are black

he touched this chair
his thick finger traced
its enamelled gold,
he touched this alabaster bottle
absent-mindedly he played
with the smooth jaws
of its hippopotamus stopper
he liked it near him
when he was tired

lots of toys
he had lots of toys
and he touched them all

years ago
he liked me near him
he touched my bare skull
I remember his soft tired hand

now
my father's hands are black.

Ceremony Of The Opening Of The Mouth

This last intimacy
with my father

this cracking open
his old mouth

has he many teeth left
for me
to break?

No breath on my hand.

The white sun.
My wet armpits.

under all the lotions
under all the perfumes
I stink
worse
than my dead father.

He's a husk
they've gutted
and dried out
with salt

I should blow him away

then, in glory,
every dawn
I'll whisper him alive
I'll be his God
his thousand-fingered
paramour
touching him everywhere
with light

his mouth
I've broken his mouth

Daddy
oh forgive me
this indecency!

In Father's Tomb

It's winter
and Theban mornings
are black ice

outside
the black is cracking
into pink and grey light

inside
I take Mother's hand
she won't talk

the rocks
in this valley
hold yesterday's Sun
like warm wells

standing by Father's
    sarcophagus
is like standing
    by a low-burning fire.

Honouring My Parents

I have just spent
seventy days
burying my father.

My mother huddles
in the stroking shade
of the temple I gave her
but shrugs off
my caresses,
her eyes
hard with grief.

When I touch her
I say
'He's not gone West,
tomorrow morning
he'll be singing in your garden
watching Aten wake up!'

She slaps me
like a woman in the market
slaps a dreaming child
'Shut up!
And do something about the Hittites!'

AKHET-ATEN

Regnal Years 12–17

The Durbar —
Year 12

Nefertiti holds my hand

our six kids stand behind us

Merytaten ogles
the loincloth bulges
of the black men

Ankhie babbling over
the cheetah on a leash
she'll want it

the little ones
rocking their pet gazelles
in their arms
drone songs like persistent crickets

gold shebu collars to reward
the officials in the procession
are waiting on their stands

the randy smell of an excited crowd

they come for my blessing
my father's gone
I'm now their only king

but my stomach is cramping!

Was the goose off
last night?
I groan
Nefertiti squeezes my hand
and points out an antelope
shivering on its lead

yes, it's lovely
I say
but does my wife feel
how frightened it is
she is squinting at it
as if she were sizing up
a vase

today
we are not feeling the same things
gifts stretch to the horizon
I'm the weary only child
given too much
for his birthday

the exuberant envoy from Kush
pushes an ostrich feather
up my nose!

Nefertiti reads my twitches
and says
don't spoil it for the children

and this time
her hand pincers mine

chariots, horses,
copper ingots . . .
thank you, thank you

and I remember
the whingeing from Tushratta
about the statues

your father promised
solid gold he said
not this gold leaf rubbish!

so what has Tushratta given
me for my durbar?

More women.
Oh, I have enough on my plate!
They'll have to play
with each other.

Nefertiti's hand is wet
but she won't let go
my gut twists around my eyes

a tame lion yawns
I look right down its throat.

Receiving
The Assyrian
Ambassadors

I can smell them
   from here.

Boiled perfume
   rising from their beards
     in cute puffs of mist.

What are they talking about?
Treaties, gold
   and Hittites.
Listening between the lines
I hear
treaties, gold and Hittites.
But I bet
they're thinking
   cold wine.

They think
   I'm laughing at them
these violent men.

The big one
   not doing the talking
has just fainted
bellyflopped
like a dropped sack of grain

he's not up to much
   slaughter
at the moment
   his face green white
like a menstruating girl.

Let them carve this
   on the terrifying walls
     of Ninevah—
their menfolk
their battle bulls
   can't take the Sun!

My Duty

I don't have a son
not even
by Kiya

does Aten prefer women?
my kingdom
prefers boys

boys of the blood

my father married
my sister Sitamun
for sons

she coped

my duty

I push it around
on the plate

which of my girls?

I'm not hungry.

My Daughter

'Daddy'
I stroke her arm
I sit up with Meketaten
my daughter
my quiet, shy girl
with a headache
   a sore throat
I hold her hand
'Daddy'
I'm here
she touches my face
it doesn't repel
   or enchant her
she just knows me
I'm her father—

'Daddy'
is she feeling well enough
   for this?
Nefertiti says no
   says she's too young
   calls me evil
   like Sobek
   snapping off young legs
   innocently fishing
   in the swamp

I'm not the crocodile god
I'm of the Sun

I don't feed in dirty water
I love her
she's well enough
I take her in my arms

she trusts me
it hurts, she shivers
I stroke her face
'Daddy'

this is for the best
        for my kingdom
I have six daughters
where else can I lay
    my seed?
My daughter
my quiet, shy girl
    goes to sleep
        in her Daddy's arms.

I was quick.
Nefertiti
    sulks in her rooms.

Shadows

Shadows
have always followed me
like starving stray dogs

as a kid
I saw at Giza
a flock of vultures
glide over
the burnished tips
   of the pyramids
while
   the sphinx
threw a shadow
   as red as a boil
that I couldn't walk round

tonight
Meki's silhouetted head
on my bedroom wall
wobbles
   like a black ripple
   in the river
because she's giggling.

Living In Truth

Meketaten died in childbirth
I'd begot
   yet another daughter.

I told them
to draw on the wall
   of her tomb
     the truth.

Draw the dead girl
draw the baby in the nurse's arms
draw me leading
   the queen into her daughter's room
to grieve and beat her brow
   behind me—

but the drawing
   was incomplete
and in parts the artist
   was sentimental—

Nefertiti
   shook off my hand
said she'd sooner
   wash in her slave's faeces
     than touch me;
went to her rooms
   locked her doors
   and her legs
against me.

I mourned alone.

But

I was a God King
I had five daughters
    and no sons,
without desire
with ice at the root of my spine
I ordered
    my servants
    to watch the underclothes
    of my third daughter,
        Ankhensenpaaten,
and tell me
    when her bleeding started.

Dawn

The full moon
in a blank sky

I itch
with lightness

then a blood ball rises
over the cowed rocks

Aten looks at Himself
in the moon

and smashes it.

Truce

'None of my girls
   are safe from you'
      my wife says

at least
we're talking

for four months
she has walked past
our bedroom

'Who's next?
Sotepenre?'

her voice rises
   on the name
      of our youngest

not loudly

but the door pushes open
   in toddles
      Sotepenre
         as if called

her hair lock
   matted
      with something sticky

she jumps in my arms
she smells
   of honeyed fig

she loves her food
too heavy
to be held for long

I put her
on the floor

'Give Mummy
    a big hug'
I tell her

I can't read
Nefertiti's white face
over our child's
    soft skull.

Just Tired

I'm just tired.

It will pass.

Letters, letters
  pestering me
  for gold or armies.
My mother's hard mouth.
The sycophants
  yawning in Aten's temple
  then elbowing for favour.
Fashion. Fashion.
My city is giddy
  with new clothes
    and scented wax.

I'm tired.
That's it.
I'm exhausted.

No wonder
Nefertiti feels heavy
  on my arm
as she sleeps
  and I stare
at the dark.

If I weren't so tired
  my spine
    wouldn't flutter
when my brother
  my wide-awake
    fire-spark Smenkhkare
      stands close.

The Splinter Bird

It's in my eye
   like a splinter

it irritates
   my attention

a mourning wheatear
   flickering on the temple floor

buzzing at the edges
   of my Hymn

Meryre's lucky
he sings about birds
   but never sees them.

Just To Talk

Evening sky.

I breast-stroke
through its pink warm air.

It eddies under
the soft cotton
of my pink-white kilt.

But my breath cuts
like a red rock face.

He's coming.
Here. In a few minutes.

Just to talk.
To tell me all about his trip
to Thebes.
The night on the river.
The women in the wine shops.
The crowds on the dock.
He'd have had fun.
I'll watch his smooth hands
talk about it all
in this pink warm air.

And my own hands
will lie still and pretend
they don't long
to touch him.

Another Daughter

She'll be your little girl,
Ankhie.

All yours.

You won't have to share her
with anyone.

Not even me.

In a few days
you'll be feeling better.

Your old self.

And you can play with her.

Your most beautiful baby.

See? Mummy was wrong.
You didn't get sick.

Meki wasn't strong.

Not like Ankhie.
Daddy's very special girl.

My brave little queen.

Ankhie's Baby

How do you tell
your twelve-year-old daughter
you're disappointed?

She's thrilled with it.

My eighth daughter,
counting Meki's blue baby
that lived for only
two minutes.

My seed spurts
nothing but girls!

I'm good for nothing
but stocking harems!

Or tombs.

Ankhie's baby
doesn't cry
her tiny hands don't grab
your hair or your thumb
her nursery is so still
you can barely hear her breathe

but Ankhie tosses her around
like a floppy doll

Nefertiti nips my arm
with her long nails

'Don't you enjoy
watching your daughters play?'

My Sleeping Brother

Asleep
Smenkhkare is cool.
And more fragrant
than melting scented wax.

I lean over him
and trail my hands
in his ripples.

But perhaps
I should stick to the safer lakes
   of Maru-Aten;
nothing is more dangerous
      for me
than swimming
   in the breath
of my sleeping brother.

Smenkhkare

Tonight
we smelt the flooding Nile

a breeze of mud
and wet donkey shit

you kissed me
on the knuckle
of my left hand

your lips nibbled
my silver ring

I can't remember
exactly
what you said

or what you were wearing
or what
    we couldn't eat

but I know
there was a sort of sunset
not worth a hymn
there was an old woman
noisy in a palace toilet
who couldn't sing

and floodwater
hanging in the air—

our perfume.

All Touch

His and my talk
is all touch.

When apart
I hallucinate
   his mouth, his eyes
and plot new ways
to touch him.

That scar on his upper lip.
I make mental notes
before I go to sleep.

I'll trace it with my thumb
ask him when it happened
take his face in my hands
bring him in close
till I feel his breath
   on my mouth

oh! the moment
when his eyes stagger!

I can't work

is my new love
my brother or my poppy juice?

Old Times

Through our garden
we walk down to the river

Sotepenre runs ahead
chasing wild kittens

every flower is open
lush with dew

my wife stops
before a head-high lotus

a cramp in the heart
I see how lovely she is

I remember pinching myself
when we were first married

what did she ever see in me?

now flood after flood
under our bridge

I can't lose her
I'd be ugly again.

Lies And Tin

'Give him something to do.'

Who?
I know who.

'He needs friends of his own age.'
my wife's voice
   peevish/old

I'm his friend!

This is dangerous,
   I love talking about him.

I wait for her to say
   his name.

Her breathing
   slow, exploratory
      in the dark

'Leave him alone.'

How can she know?

I pull her into my arms
she cuddles up
   out of habit
I kiss her short fine hair
I've always liked her
   without her wig

she sighs,
   kisses my neck

'Do you love me?'

I answer
with hands, murmurs
   and nibble her ears

she pulls away
she won't play

I can't see her eyes.

'For all of our sakes
send him to Kush!'

my old snake
doesn't say please

'I can't stand it
    can't stand it.'

neither can I

I give her lies
I give her tin.

Ebony Cats

I preen and snigger
  when he talks to me
  when he looks at me
    like that.

His eyes are almonds.
I twitch
  to pluck them out
and eat them
instead
  I play
  like one of my kids
with the ebony cats on the table
my fingers
    silly.

Touch me, he whispers
touch me, he insists
I froth at the mouth
swallow my tongue

where has the Good God gone?

helpless
I see the crops black
  up and down the river.

Little Brother

Smenkhkare, please,
go back to your own bed—

no,
   I'm not moralising
no,
   scales, crocodiles
   and jackals preaching in the Underworld
   don't scare me—
   priests' bullshit!

yes,
   you're more gorgeous
   than any woman in the Black Land
yes,
   I'm amazed
   your boring older brother
   makes you so randy

but
   I can't see you, my darling,
and
   I don't like fucking in the dark.

The Last Straw

Last night
in some boiling hour
Ankhie's baby died

Nefertiti thought I was up
watching for Aten
in the garden

she came
to see if Smenkhkare
knew where I was

I was in his arms

she grabbed the pitcher
by the bed
drenching us awake
with warm wine

'Your daughter's dead'
she said

Ankhie!

I ran down the hall naked
dripping wine

'Wrong daughter!'
she said

this afternoon
she took Ankhie
and the others

she left the dead baby
with me.

She Said Look In The Mirror

She told me to look
   in the mirror.

She was leaving.

I wouldn't see a God
   she said
I'd see myself
I'd see why she was leaving.

She is my mirror.

I saw
   Meki's face outlined in mummy cloths

I saw
   with a pitiless indecency
      Smenkhkare's heaving hips
         as he comes in my mouth

My dead daughter
my debauched little brother

oh! my love!
you know me better

that is not your king
that is not your man

look in the mirror
   she said
you will see yourself
you will see why
   I am leaving.

She Leaves Her Things

What sort of face
   is she wearing
   at the Northern Palace?

She's left behind
   all her cosmetics.
Even her tweezers.
Will my love be sprouting
   thick eyebrows?

Grow hideous, Nefertiti,
tumble in public
your hairy grief
like a performing dwarf.

Even Hapu. The monkey pot.
Left him behind too.
I see the mark
   of your finger nail
in his kohl.

I stole him
   from my mother's chest,
we were still kids
   but your new breasts
      nudged me to it.

I'd like one like that,
   you said
so I pinched him.
Hapu
   we called him
after the smart little monkey
   who built temples
      for my father.

I'm not touching your things.

Not looking at myself
in your mirror.

The sluts in my harem
can have the lot.

Ma'at

Mother,
   Creation always begins
   with the wish
   with the act
     of a god.

Even in the priests' yarn
   old Ptah
had to start
   somewhere.

Remember
   the first ma'at
     was chaos!

Look at my city.
Is it a blasphemous shambles?
Shaped by the sky
   and the valley
it is a true temple,
you can breathe it
   like you can drink
     the Nile.

Living things, Mother,
   I make living things.

Your ma'at is a sarcophagus.
My ma'at is life!

In My Own Time

It wasn't the same
    with Nefertiti.

There are no poems
    to describe
holding your own brother
    in your arms.

No, I'm not going to write one
    right this minute.

I know I wrote plenty
    for her,
carved her cartouche
like flowering graffiti
all over my city.

I promise
you won't miss out.

I'll tell the Two Lands
    all about you
    in my own time, sweetheart.

That Hawk

We're not kids, Smenkhkare.

Of course that hawk
is beautiful!
You can watch
its shadow skimming
the desert sand
like a featherlight stone.

Just don't give it legs
don't dress it up in a kilt
don't make it absurd
with a god's name
and a stinking tomb
in the hills
for thieves to piss in.

It's a hawk, not Horus,
It's a hawk
it's not you
it's not me
I'm the Good King
it couldn't be.

It has its own fiery heart

Don't ask me to tear it out
to worship and douse!

Bandaged Pets

The priests teach
the timid, the superstitious
   and the sentimental
(almost everyone)
to give pathetic presents
   to Osiris.

Poor bugger.
Where does he keep
   all those bandaged cats?
Meowing furiously for what?
   Bandaged fish?

He must wish sometimes
he'd stayed dismembered
instead
   he was glued together
to mind other people's
   hungry, rotting pets
     for eternity.

Borders

Mother, tell this
to the bigots and the priests

in sex and art
I'm like a Hittite army
I don't recognise borders

I heap male and female
into one silky dune
and dig in my toes.

My Heir

Next Inundation feast
when the water is high
Smenkhkare will marry
my eldest daughter

he says
it won't make
any difference to us

he grins

'Don't be jealous!
Meri is just like her mother
without her mother's looks

she knows
I can't be king
without her

she knows
I can't marry you, big brother.'

Smenkhkare's Wedding

I'm watching her
  not him

Why didn't I geld him?

Instead I gilded him
  my gold man
  my
    little king.

Marriage.
    The word puckers my mouth
    like a hen's arse.

His marriage.

Her earrings.
They wink
    like a dancing girl's.

Chipping Her Out

My eyes hurt as I write

it's my own fault

this morning
I woke up
my wife's name in my mouth
like last night's garlic

she might as well still be here
like a bloody fish hook in my thumb

instead
she's whooping it up
at the Northern Palace
on my furniture
on my gold plate
with my best servants
and all my children
except Merytaten

while I float woozily
on cups of wine and beer
through the copper life here

this morning
I kept spitting
in the garden

but nothing would make my mouth
sweet

so I grabbed a chisel
and went down
to my wife's old kiosk
by the river
the air was prickly
with the scent of lotus

I was giddy
no Ahmose and his big cool fan

just the weight
of a chisel
in my hand

then
with the swings
of a temple butcher
I chipped out Nefertiti's face
from her stela

I was blacker
than a fit

the rock
sprayed white dust
into my eyes

my eyes hurt as I write.

My Invitations

Aten, this morning
there were only twenty people
in the temple

I felt like a host
at a party
surrounded by columns
of uneaten food,
vats of undrunk wine,
unoccupied musicians
scratching their crotches
and the pity of those who came.

My invitations to Your feast
are ignored

or worse, feared,
as if a summons
to a blasphemous orgy

this morning
all that silent space
where the buzzing of a fly
gorging on the offal
of the sacrifice
was louder
than the singing of the Hymn.

Aten,
    it's your turn
    to send out the invitations

and this time
    insist.

Moorhens

Moorhens hurrying
  through the sunset on the water

I grab at them
  like I'd grab for a drink

Bliss!
I'm not their king

the Hittites aren't threatening
their peace
Aten isn't threatening
their reed and water gods

we don't need to know
or understand each other

I am not their prison
or salvation.

Them

I'm not asking them
   to stare at Aten

go blind
   for my sake

but look at them

they cluster on Amun
like flies on a dead ram's eye
   and suck hard

Aten loves them
I don't

I'm just asking them
   to suck
      on the Light.

Nefertiti

Nefertiti, Nefertiti
testing that spell again
no, nothing
    nothing happens.
I remember
    tasting that name
        in my mouth.
A name wobbly on its lovely stem
    as innocent, as intoxicating
        as a poppy field.

I'm a God. She was a husk.
I dreamed her up
and ordered her dream
    for the whole of my kingdom.

In the end
    she smelt of tears
        and tar

I tore away

for my own choices
    my own will.

Ordering Her Dream

Without her wig
she was her most beautiful
I wanted to make her simple
and give to the world
its first goddess
with a clear woman's face
not a cat
not a cow.

The Two Lands had never seen a queen.
Hatshepsut wore
a beard
Nefertiti
wore the blue crown.

I ordered her dream
in sculpture
in tomb painting
in her cartouche entwined with mine.

Blue she glowed
like the lotus flower
opening in the morning
to push out the head
of the newborn Sun.

Vicious
Memories

It takes a few drinks
before I can talk
to my eldest daughter

even with the balcony
tilted into the evening breeze
and the flowers opening
on the table

she sips at her wine
as if it were lemon juice

but as the night
gets silkier
she nuzzles her cup
until her nose disappears

it's then
I ask after her mother

'She's fine.'

How often do you visit?

'When she needs me.'

How are things at the Northern Palace?

'They're all well.'

I order more wine.
Strong aromatic stuff
from Crete.

My daughter takes
a long drink
until she burps

Pa overfills my cup
giggling
as the wine floods
across the table.

I order him away.

How's married life?

She drains her cup
her hand is shaking.

Are you happy with Smenkhkare?

'Does it matter?
He had to marry me
didn't he?'

Don't recite statecraft
to your own father!

Are you happy?

'Is there any more wine?'

Are you happy?

She tips up her cup
it's empty

'I don't like fucking
my uncle
any more than I liked fucking
you.'

Only twice!
Little girls
have such vicious memories.

I take my time
finishing my wine

and tell her

'You don't know how much
I miss my Meki.'

No Fun Anymore

Smenkhkare says
I've got no sense of humour

I'm boring
he says
I get drunk
and talk about my kids
I blubber
over Ankhie's
blue wooden hippo
with its rows of yellow teeth
set in a yawn

Smenkhkare stepped on it
and laughed

the terrible crack
as he broke the back
of that old toy

I know
I've got no sense of humour.

Mother's
Noseless Thief

Mother twitches
Mother stares at the floor
Mother shows her teeth

because I'm here
because I'm pulling my randy cow face
(Pa reckons my Hathor impersonation
is hysterical!)
because my neck is thin
because my lips are thick
because I am not her beautiful little bull

Mother would swap me
and all my Aten gold
for a noseless thief
who worshipped his mother
who made sober and dishonest statues
of himself, his wife and his soul.

For Mother
shall I be the good family man
with his scabby hand slithering
through the death reek of mummy cloths
for amulets
on the quiet?

On the quiet, on the quiet
that's where my Mummy lives

Well,
    fuck you, Mother
I'd rather be on the nose.

Wants

It's not working, brother.

It's an effort.

On some evenings
    before you come to my bed
I sigh

sigh
    like a criminal
        hacking out copper
            in the Sinai

you don't bore me
your body is too exciting
    like holding a rippling snake
        in my bare hand

but your mind is young
    and dull

it trots beside me
    like a fat puppy

I long to gallop
    the horses of the Sun
and dust the world
    with my thundering light

you want
    to beat me at senet
you want
    to bag ducks in the reeds
    with your moronic mates

you want
    to wrestle or spear
    anything that moves
you want
    to flash your big prick
    in every brothel
    up and down the river!

You want me
   to clap your kills
you want me
   to stop nagging you
   with the wonder of Aten.

We're both wanting, brother.

Sheep Of Thebes

Mother, I hate Thebes
it's a priests' hole

you can keep Amun's Paradise
all those sheep heads

fitting that Amun
is a sheep

his priests
baaing in their dark pen
at Karnak

baa baa baa
throw all those silly bastards
in their Sacred Lake

fill their woolly heads
with water

you're not tethering me
there

no ponce
in a leopard skin
is going to baa
sheepshit at me

Mother, stop your blubbering
my head is sore
from a long day
singing to Aten

all right, take Smenkhkare,
let the priests baa at him

he's good at dozing
with his eyes open.

Dirty Feet

Smenkhkare is in Thebes
but I don't miss him

what do we have left?

Skin.

My room stinks.
Is there shit
on my sandals?

I'm always washing
my feet.

Sycophants And Soldiers

No one walks straight
  around me

sycophants and soldiers
  all give their bellies
  a deep crease

they can't look in my face
I can't talk to them

they are my slabs of granite
my roof
my wall

I can't look out

they make
  the sort of temple
  my father liked

a mortuary temple.

The Small Room

There's a room I saw in a dream
I had ordered someone to take me there
the walls were closing in
I had been buried alive

I thought of the rooms in old pyramids
I would never build one
I thought of the rooms in deep tombs
built like rats' holes in the cliffs
tombs like my father's
I didn't want one
no walls would ever close on me
I would not die to darkness
and a small room

so I designed my own tomb
with straight lines
so the Sun could follow me

in my dream
in that small room
there was a black smell
burning bandages
viscera from smashed canopic urns,
on the floor, in the oily flames,
someone was burning my mummy
and obliterating me.

Amun's
Blessing

Amun got him.

My boy.

Wound him in cloths
of fever and pus.

And choked him dead.

Mother, I listened to you.

Send Smenkhkare, you said.
The priests don't hate him.

Do they hate me, Mother?

Have I ever given them
cause?

Did I shit in their temple?
Did I piss in their Lake?

I let Karnak stand.

Sometimes
I dreamt it
black and brittle

a carcass
under the rays of Aten

but no
I am not a vulture

I don't tear at
stenching old gods

I let Karnak stand, Mother

and listened to you.

Amun has sent the plague
you said
the city is heaving
and wailing
everyone blames you
do something
send Smenkhkare
to make peace with Amun.

I did.
I let my boy go.

Amun took him
into his pestilent sanctuary
and blessed him.

Now, Mother,
it's your turn
to listen.

Tell your friends
at Karnak
they'll have to move
fast
to hide their filthy god
from my blessing!

Scarab

Will I stop eating?
Starve
and find your shadow
to snuggle.

Will I tell the musicians
to shut up?
Walk through that cobweb
of silence
and have your voice
stick to my face.

Smenkhkare.
I can't move.
Make decisions for me.

Or leave me properly.
Not this tease.

Are you really dead?
Let me sniff your embalmed
hands.
Let me open your canopic
urns.
Give me your still heart.
It will be my scarab.

You can't separate
a heart
from its brother.

Your Name
(Burial Poem)

Smenkhkare, my queen,
I bury you
but not your beauty

your sweet breath
will live forever
in my breath
saying your name.

Give me your hands
so I can hold your spirit

and grow beautiful
saying your name.

The Gods

You
   lumps of mud
you
   carved sticks
you
   globs of gold
you
   crude kiddies' nightmare
you
   pathetic distortion
   of beautiful animals!

I am cracking
   the Sun's whip

I will be this kingdom's
   most wonderful enema

but don't expect
   some quack's purge
      from me

I know my poisons.

My favourite works like an acid.

I'll feed it
   to all your names.

Its name?
Oblivion.

Plague

Plague is like an idol
in a secret room

it anoints itself
in the dark.

Until the day
perfumed with pus
carried on the shoulders
of its maggot priests

it arrives.

My little one
my youngest
Sotepenre
has just dropped her head
to kiss its feet.

Sticks And Stones

Mother died cold sober.

Not even plague
could make her
bleed gibberish.

She wouldn't take
my hand.

'Seth!'
she called me

pervert
god-killer Seth

it wasn't the moment
to debate Mother

sticks and stones
I thought

'Seth!' she hissed
and pulled back
the slimy sheet

her breasts caked
in black sores

I looked out the window
at the huge white noon sun

oh, my Father,
boil the river dry
and swallow me alive!

Mother sent her slaves away.
I've always been a good son.
She had the last word.

'Tutmose.'

The Party's Over

Ay carried out my orders.

He smashed Amun's name
from the highest obelisk
in Thebes.

He scratched away
Amun's name
from Mother's perfume bottle.

He was thorough.

Today he dealt with me
thoroughly.

He looked me in the eyes.
He didn't bow.

'The party's over,'
he said
and poured himself
a drink.

'The Hittites
have eaten Mitanni.

It's disappeared.

Our vassals are
on their backs
like raped women.

Your soldiers
are too busy looting
on your behalf
to bother
with fighting.

Horemheb will whip them
into line.

Our family,
apart from Ankhie and Tut,
are jostling each other
in the tomb.

They've died too fast
for much elbow room.

You're our Plague.

I have the cure.

Tut will be king.
Amun's king.

The party's over
you've always been imaginative
find your own way out.'

Hard And Healthy

I haven't had a fit
for months

only bottomless headaches

I look well
my nails grow
hard and healthy

I'm putting on weight

am I the Plague?

A Gift From
My Wife

Why are you so generous to me?

Our hair filthy with ash
our eyes wrecked with mourning
we pour each other wine
and toast Aten

from childhood on
you taught me
to live in the Light
to take on the world

but it was you
Aten lit up

remember
that winter afternoon
in the Western Desert
when you stopped the driver
to look at the pink alabaster
shining
in ridges across the sand

you walked back
with a piece for me

it was warm from your hand

why are you so generous to me?

Doctor Skull-Opener

Floodtime

that hurting
old smell!

The water
licking the temple walls

but my orders are out
the peasants
can stay
growing mould
in their damp houses

no more building
no more temples
no more holy work

I won't have Aten
insulted
in stone monstrosities
mud-slapped together
where His name
and mine
are shat on!

the water licks
and stinks
at the base of my skull

it rises
every day
it rises
like a filthy tide
in my eyes

I can taste
its scumming froth
I can taste
its floating rot

laughing doves
flit
with soft colours
in the palms

I can't hear them

I can't come out
of this fit

tomorrow Pentu,
my Skull-Opener,
will come

he will clean
his instruments
in the sacred fire

he will give me
poppy juice

his knife will free
this muck

tomorrow
Aten will burn back
through the fresh air
sweet
in my empty skull.

Goodbye To
Akhet-Aten

You have been my
most constant lover

even in despair
I will not be mute
before you

all these years
you have curved around me
my own city
like a jewelled water snake

I have worn you
and glistened inside
your watchful beauty

I'm leaving you
because I have no choice

I can't stop
what they will do
to you

I can't watch you die too

my singing days
are dust
so I talk to you
by the river

please accept
this scrappy goodbye
as my thanks

for the years
we had together
when we were
imperishably marvellous.

Epilogue— Eternal Life

At Sunrise
the souls bolt from their tombs
and fly as birds
in chorusing clouds
around me

my presence
is as agitating
as a honey-cake in the Sun
to foraging bees

these starving ghosts
salivate in my aroma of Light

I open their eyes
but I won't stuff their bellies

the workmen of the new king
have arrived with chisels
and hammers
they have orders
to cut down my city
and cut out my name

but Ramesses can't cut down the Sun
or cut out all the birds
in the dawn sky
who call and call

my name
and teach it to their
gaping nestlings

Akhenaten. Akhenaten.

Their wings ripple about my ears
in raucous rainbows.

Akhenaten. Akhenaten.

Their eyes are pestering white prisms.

Why does eternal life
make us so ravenous?

NOTES ON CHARACTERS

(Almost all are historical)

Ahmose Fan-bearer.

Akhenaten King of Egypt from 1378 BC. to 1362 BC. Second son of Amunhotep III, ruler of Egypt's Eighteenth Dynasty of Kings.

Amunhotep III Father of Akhenaten. Ruled over a magnificent court at Thebes.

Ankhesenpaaten (Ankhie) Third daughter, after Akhenaten's death married to Tutankhamun.

Any Royal secretary (a very old man].

Ay Queen Tiy's brother and Nefertiti's father who served Akhenaten in the military post of Master of the Horse. Pharaoh on the death of Tutankhamun.

Bek Akhenaten's sculptor whom he instructed in the new style.

Hatshepsut A previous 18th dynasty pharaoh—a Queen who ruled in her own right, dressing in the male insignia of power including the false beard.

Horemheb General, Pharaoh on Ay's death. He began the execration of Akhenaten.

Kiya Favourite wife of Akhenaten's harem.

Meketaten (Meki) Second daughter, died in childbirth.

Meryre High priest of the Great Temple of Aten at Akhet-Aten.

Merytaten (Meri) Eldest daughter, married to Smenkhkare.

Neferneferuaten-ta-sherit Fourth daughter.

Neferneferure Fifth daughter.

Nefer-re Priest in the temple of Re-Herakhte at Heliopolis.

Nefertiti Akhenaten's cousin, Chief Wife and Queen.

Nofret Akenhaten's pet tabby cat.

Parenefer (Pa) Cup-bearer.

Penehse A royal attendant.

Pentu Royal doctor.

Ramesses Ramesses II, a bellicose and grandiose pharaoh who used the ruins of Akhet-Aten as a quarry for his own temples and statues.

Smenkhkare Akhenaten's younger brother. His parents were probably Tiy and Amunhotep III. In the last year of Akhenaten's reign he was co-ruler.

Sotepenre Sixth and youngest daughter.

Tiy Mother of Akhenaten. Chief wife of Amunhotep III.

Tushratta King of ancient Mitanni, a very anxious and demanding ally of Egypt's during this period.

Tutankhamun (Tut) Changed his name from Tutankhaten after Akhenaten's death. Youngest son of Tiy and Amunhotep III. Youngest brother of Akhenaten, succeeded him on the throne after his death.

Tutmose Akhenaten's elder brother who died prematurely.

NOTES FOR THE POEMS

I Survived [p.3]
'Amun'. A god whose powerful cult was temporarily displaced by the deity of Aten.

Mother's New God [p.11]
'Leopard Spots'. The High Priest of Amun wore a leopard skin. 'Mut'. Goddess. Wife of Amun.

Heliopolis [p.14]
'Herakhte'. A name of Re—the sun god of Heliopolis.

Amun's Sactuary [p.17]
'Horus-in-Waiting'. The kings of Egypt saw themselves as incarnations of Horus—the falcon sun god.

My Fifteenth Birthday [p.18]
'Senet'. A board game popular among Egyptians.

My Co-Regency Coronation [p.23]
'Droning flies of Memphis'. Coronation ceremonies were traditionally held in Memphis, the ancient capital of Egypt. Akhenaten had little respect for ceremonies that were not of his own initiation.

Like No One Else [p.26]
'The Two Lands'. A common expression used by Egyptians for Upper and Lower Egypt. Egypt itself they called 'Kemet'—its habitable Nile Valley, 'the Black Land', the desert wastes beyond, 'the Red Land'.

Fits [p.28]
'Ka'. The immortal spirit.

My White Queen p.30
'Sistrum'. A musical instrument—something like a rattle—often shown on

158

stela being shaken by Nefertiti and Akhenaten's two eldest daughters in Aten worship.

God-Watching [p.33].
'Thoth'. The god of writing and the moon. Depicted as an ibis or a baboon.

My Ka [p.34]
'Kush'. The Lower Sudan.

Inundation [p.41]
The essential months when the Nile flooded, fertilising the fields. During this period there were religious festivals and the peasantry, largely unemployed, were drafted into a labour force for public works.

Hymn to the Sun [p.46]
A famous composition of Akhenaten's. I am grateful to Winton Thomas' English translation published in 'Documents from Old Testament Times', which I have reworked.

My Way [p.52]
'Window of Appearances'. The state balcony of the royal palace at Akhet-Aten, from where Akhenaten and Nefertiti threw down gifts to reward their followers.

Hoopoe [p.55]
A common African crested bird, popular as a pet and as an artistic motif.

Sauce [p.57]
'Osiris'. The god of the Underworld and of vegetation, symbolising in his death and rebirth the rise and fall of the Nile and the growth of grain. Egyptians saw in the Osirian rites their own rebirth after death.

Death and a Randy Vulture [p.69]
'Eset'. Another name for Isis. Wife and sister of Osiris. Mother of Horus. The great Egyptian goddess of fertility and magic.

Ankhie's Lion [p.74]
'Sekhmet'. The lion-headed goddess of war and pestilence.

The Durbar [p.87]
A public audience with a large gathering of representatives from vassal states and the great powers in Asia, Africa and the Aegean bearing gifts for Akhenaten on his accession to sole rule following the death of his father.

My Daughter [p.92]
'Sobek'. The crocodile god.

Living In Truth   [p.95
Literally 'Living in Ma'at'—one of Akhenaten's royal titles.

Truce   [p.98
'Hair lock'. Before puberty Egyptian children had shaved heads with one
side lock of hair.

Just Tired   [p.100
'Scented wax'. Wax cone head ornaments were worn at parties. They would
melt fragrantly over the head and shoulders of the wearer.

My Sleeping Brother   [p.105
'Maru-Aten'. A temple with a pleasure lake on the southern outskirts of
Akhet-Aten.

Ebony Cats   [p.111
'The Good God'. The common name for the king.

Ma'at   [p.117
Central to the Egyptians' view of kingship. A concept of universal order,
truth and harmony—the responsibility of the king. 'Ptah' The god of cre-
ation.

Mother's Noseless Thief   [p.134
'Hathor'. The horned cow-goddess of love.

Sheep of Thebes   [p.137
Amun was often depicted as a ram. The avenue of sphinxes at Karnak have
rams' heads.

Your Name   [p.144
'Burial Poem'. Smenkhkare was buried in a coffin that had originally been
made for a queen or a princess. This poem was found on the coffin. I have
reworked it from Sir Alan Gardiner's translation (Journal of Egyptian
Archaeology).

Sticks And Stones   [p.147
'Seth'. A powerful god associated with disorder, sterility, homosexuality, th
desert and thunder.

Doctor Skull-Opener   [p.152
'Skull-opening'. A trepanning operation performed by Egyptian doctors.
More often fatal than not.

Epilogue   [p.155
'Eternal Life'. Akhenaten claimed that he would look after his followers in
the afterworld. He believed the dead came to life with the rising sun.